EUREKA MILL

Eureka Mill

poems

Ron Rash

HUB CITY PRESS
SPARTANBURG, SC

Library of Congress Cataloging-
in-Publication Data

Rash, Ron, 1953- author.
Eureka Mill : poems / Ron Rash.
Spartanburg SC : Hub City Press, [2018]
LCCN 2018007160 | ISBN 9781938235443
LCC PS3568.A698 A6 2018 | DDC 811/.54—dc23
LC record available at https://lccn.loc.
gov/2018007160

Book design: Meg Reid
Proofreader: Kalee Lineberger and
Katie Moulton
Printed in Dexter, MI by Thomson-Shore
Cover Photo © Mark Robinson
"Textile Mill Top Floor"

TEXT Caslon Thirty ITC 10.5 / 15

Hub City Press gratefully acknowledges support from the Chapman
Cultural Center and the National Endowment for the Arts.

186 W. Main Street
Spartanburg, SC 29306
864-327-8515
www.hubcity.org

for my children, James and Caroline, and in memory of my grandparents, James Moody Rash and Mary Lee Miller Rash

Table of Contents

Foreword

AFTER THE CIVIL WAR MANY TEXTILE MILLS WERE moved from New England to the South to be nearer to the source of cotton. Also the mill owners sought to take advantage of much cheaper labor in a region where there was little competing industry. There were also former plantation owners and Confederate officers ruined by the war who hoped to recover their fortunes by building new cotton mills. Many owners of the mills were addressed as Colonel.

In the late nineteenth century most of the employees in the mills, always white, were local citizens grateful for jobs in an area devastated by the late war. By the early twentieth century word of the job opportunities in the mills had spread to the mountains, and many who lived on failing farms there began to migrate to the cotton mill towns, hoping to trade the uncertainties of farming for the promise of steady wages. The poor farms on the ridges were worn out by erosion and years of mono-cropping with corn, and the farmers were eager to trade the struggles of farming for a dependable income.

Floods, drought, hailstorms, pests, diseases, and faraway markets made their lives on small holdings a losing gamble.

The mountain folk were grateful for the work, and the mill owners and managers encouraged an atmosphere of community and family in the mill towns, providing cheap houses for rent, credit at the company stores, Christmas parties and gifts for the children, picnics, and sponsoring baseball teams to play other company towns. As a result there was loyalty to the companies, and to the owners personally, as husbands and wives, aunts and uncles, grandparents, and small children, worked long hours in the mill.

Though working hard for low wages, most still viewed themselves as landed people, descended from the first settlers. Out of necessity they might be working in the mills, but that just was temporary. What the mill workers refused to admit was that their move to the mills was a one-way journey. Many had lost their farms, or sold their land for a pittance. They would never go back to the ridges, but they held tenaciously to the idea of themselves as people of the land and of the hills.

However they preferred to see themselves, the mill hands were indeed trapped in their new lives. Wages were low, the hours long, and there was little chance to escape the paternalistic system of the mill economy. In fact, there was no other place for them to go, especially after the Great Depression hit the area.

Ron Rash's *Eureka Mill*, published two decades ago, is a landmark in Appalachian writing. In poem after poem he recreates the lives and memories of those who came down out of the hills to labor in the mills and became accustomed to a new way of life as "lintheads." *Eureka Mill* was a breakthrough in the portrayal of life in the textile village, and of the people who left their land to work for wages. In free verse, dramatic monologues, blank verse, terse

verse narratives, ballads, and elegiac lyrics, Rash brings to life the
voices and stories of a forgotten community, almost a century ago.

Eureka Mill begins with an "Invocation" which the poet con-
cludes by addressing his grandfather who left the land to work in
the mill.

> Grandfather guide my hand
> to weave with words a thread
> of truth as I write down
> your life and other lives,
> close kin but strangers too,
> those lives all lived as gears
> in Springs' cotton mill
> and let me not forget
> your lives were more than that.

Poems such as "Tobacco" and "In a Dry Time" evoke the long
labor, the harsh uncertainties of life on mountain farms. The latter
poem ends:

> I had no harvest to pay my bills.
> So tried for another loan and when
> the bank said sorry I begged but still
> it did no good, though my eyes filled
> with water, too little water to mend
> broken crops dead in the field.
> I left crop rows for rows of steel.

But *Eureka Mill* is not all about misery and loss. Poems such as
"Low Water" record the good times and humor of mill town life.
When water in the river fell below a certain point in drought, the

mill would shut down temporarily, giving the workers a much relished break.

> There was nothing else that Colonel Springs could do
> but let us go, at least a little while.

> Out in the yard someone would play guitar.
> We'd sing "Rock of Ages" or some other hymn,
> or sleep until the water gained up again,
> and the whistle blew and we'd have to go back in.

Poems such as "Spring Fever" present the intense nostalgia many mill hands felt for the farm life they had left. At planting time they ached for the fresh-turned fields, forgetting the loneliness and defeat of that way of life. Other poems tell of the dangers of mill work. In "Accident" a woman loses part of her hair and scalp caught in a speed frame, but returns to work later the same day: "She didn't want to lose a half day's wage."

Sometimes men got drunk on Saturday nights in the mill towns and were killed in fights, as in the poem "Preparing the Body." At times during the Great Depression the people ate squirrels, which they called "Hoover hogs." "Flying Squadrons" of union organizers were attacked and beaten up. One of the most trenchant poems is "The Ballad of Ella Mae Wiggins," about the laborer and folk singer who, because of her support for the union, was killed by strike breakers or the owner's thugs in September of 1929.

> They shot her in the chest and let her die,
> then took her body into town.
> She was just a linthead on this earth

but in heaven she'll wear a crown.
We won't forget the day
strikebreakers struck poor Ella Mae down.

One of the many risks of working in the cotton mills was the disease called "Brown Lung." Even after being shifted to jobs outside the mill the sufferer found it difficult to recover lung capacity. The disablement was permanent.

Sometimes I'd spend the whole night coughing up
what I'd been breathing in all day at work.
I'd sleep in a chair or take a good stiff drink,
Anything to get a few hours rest.

Eureka Mill is in the tradition of *Spoon River Anthology*. Rash lets many of his characters tell their own stories in dramatic monologues. One of the most memorable is "Last Interview" in which a mill owner recalls his career and explains himself. The poem reminds us a little of Robert Browning's "My Last Duchess." The mill owner says to the interviewer:

You'll slant what I have said to fit your needs.
I know how writers work, their luxury
of always being outside looking in,
passing easy judgments while they risk
nothing of their own, mere dilettantes.
Your words mean nothing to me. I know the truth.
I gave them more than they ever had before.

Other outstanding poems include "The Famous Photographer Visits Eureka," spoken by a child laborer, after the photographer exposed the shame of children put to work in the unsafe mills. The speaker resists seeing her life merely in the stark terms of the photographer's campaign.

"Revival" tells of the threats of hell heard from the evangelical pulpit. But the speaker observes that he and all his fellow workers must have sinned grievously before to have ended up in the hell of the cotton mill.

> We laughed that night but later there were times,
> when we were sweating in the cotton mill,
> we'd try our best to remember another life,
> and what bad things we'd done to end up here.

"1934" is another poem about the resistance of the workers, under the watchful eye of the mill owner, to the efforts of union organizers.

> When a flying squadron headed south
> and crossed the Chester County line,
> we left our shift to walk outside.
> We filled our fists to welcome them.

The poem "Listening to WBT" is a testimony to the relish and joy music on the radio brought to the people, and the way the songs expressed their own hopes and the harsh truths of their lives.

> Maybe it was the banjo and guitar,
> the way they prettied up the words,
> that made those songs lighten up your heart
> with a deep-water Baptist hymn.

Or maybe in the end it was the words,
the bare-assed truth making a stand
in a voice that could have been your own.

The most moving poem in *Eureka Mill* is probably "July, 1949." It
is the story of Ron Rash's mother, who as a young woman drops
her hoe in a mountain field to run to a waiting car and ride with
relatives to the Piedmont to work in a cotton mill.

She is dreaming another life,
young enough to believe
it can only be better—
indoor plumbing, eight-hour shifts, a man
who waits unknowing for her, a man
who cannot hear through the weave room's
roar the world's soft click,
fate's tumblers falling into place,
soft as the sound of my mother's
bare feet as she runs,
runs toward him, toward me.

Ron Rash has won many honors for his short stories and novels,
but none of his published work is more significant or satisfying
than the poems of *Eureka Mill*, which illuminate an almost forgot-
ten corner of Southern and Appalachian history and lives.

—Robert Morgan

Author's Note

WHEN EUREKA COTTON MILL WAS TORN DOWN IN 2014, I salvaged a brick taken from the rubble. I keep it as a talisman of sorts and a reminder that my life, the possibility of my life, began when my father and mother, a farm girl from the North Carolina mountains, met at the mill in 1948. Eureka's demise was no exception. At the end of the last century, the South's cotton mills were almost all shut down, the mill villages that surrounded them fast becoming ghost towns. Except for those who had worked in these mills, few seemed to notice. *Eureka Mill* was an attempt to keep some memory of that culture alive, so I am particularly pleased that the volume retains enough of a readership to merit a new edition.

But *Eureka Mill* is also a way to honor my father's grandparents, who would work at the mill a while, then go back to live in the North Carolina mountains, only to return to Eureka for the mill's steadier pay. My grandparents wanted a better life for my father and he achieved that better life. Though he dropped out of high school to work at Eureka, my father eventually received a GED. In his mid twenties, while still working at the mill, he went to night school and earned a college degree. My mother got her college degree in her early forties, and became, like my father, a teacher. So *Eureka Mill* honors her as well. They gave me opportunities my grandparents, especially my illiterate grandfather, could not have dreamed of. Whatever merit these poems have is the is the gift of their labors.

—Ron Rash

He moved to the mill village. There was only one condition attached. He and children who worked were expected to work in the mill. That is all. And that is enough. That makes the house a spiritual grave and the mill village a spiritual cemetery. It buries its inhabitant and hides them from the world.

—Frank Tannenbaum, *Darker Phases of the South*

Invocation

This late night I spread
a fraying Springmaid bedsheet
across the kitchen table.
In the almost silence
of house-creak and time's
persistent tracking of eternity,
I unscrew the mason jar,
pool the lid with moonshine
flare the battered cigarette lighter.
A blue trembling rises from liquid
expanding finally to smoke,
all elements merging tonight,
whispering out the window,
curling northward to seep six feet
into the black bony dirt
and guide his spirit across
the declining mountains to this room,
where I sit and sip, await
a tobacco-breathed haint, shadowless shadow,
bloodless blood-kin I have summoned
to hear my measured human prayer:
> *Grandfather guide my hand*
> *to weave with words a thread*
> *of truth as I write down*
> *your life and other lives,*
> *close kin but strangers too,*
> *those lives all lived as gears*
> *in Springs' cotton mill*
> *and let me not forget*
> *your lives were more than that.*

I

Eureka

Here was no place   for illumination
the cotton dust thick   window-strained light.
The metal squall drowned   what could not be shouted
everything geared   warping and filling.

Though surely there were   some times that he paused
my grandfather thinking   *This is my life*
and catching himself   before he was caught
lost wages or fingers   the risk of reflection.

Or another recalled   in those reckoning moments
remembering the mountains   the hardscrabble farm
where a workday as long   bought no guarantee
of money come fall   full bellies in winter.

To earn extra pay   each spring he would climb
the mill's water tower   repaint one word.
That vowel-heavy word   defined the horizon
a word my grandfather   could not even read.

Drought

We raised only dust
that July, rubbed knees
raw in church, in pastures
praying for one gorged cloud
that never came.
So remembered the old way.
Blacksnakes we'd shared
barns with years
fleshed our barbed wire fences.
Their hoe-hacked heads sparkled
with clots of flies.
Each day we walked our fields,
death stained any breeze
like overripe berries,
like the festering seed
of our faithlessness.
We smelled what was coming—
the speckled trout rotting
in the cracked creekbeds,
the heat-killed hogs
and chickens of August.
When the first snow finally fell
and we'd gathered what God
had spared us, mortgaged
our farms for the rest,
we listed in the barndark
to rats eating the grain.

They did not fear us.
What they feared
was now bleached bones
rattling in the wind.

Tobacco

Before the dream of tobacco, golden
as it cured inside our October barns,
we had thought our land generous enough,
the apple trees drooping their fruit to our hands,
the woods and streams thick with rabbit and trout.
We planted our oats and corn and wheat and beans.
Some crops were lost but the springhouse filled
with enough to carry us through the winter.
But then the fence laws passed and taxes rose.
We needed money crops to keep our farms.
We heard the legends of those who had no more
land than us but now were men of ease,
who lived in the columned houses tobacco raised,
and knew if they are rich then we were poor,
and so tobacco came and our world changed.
We bought those bitter seeds, the fertilizer,
the poison for the worms. In January
we set out plant beds and later broke
the best ground in our bottomlands. Then came
the kind of toil we'd never known before,
plowing, chopping, suckering, and topping.
We left the beans and corn unhoed, let weeds
strangle our other fields, the apple trees
unpruned in the orchard as we spent
the days kneeling to tobacco, cupping
our blistered hands around the plants
as though each leaf were a small, green flame
a summer breeze might snuff.

By fall some blight or drought or sudden rain
had wiped out all our crop or most of it.
When a good year came that only meant
everybody else had done as well,
so prices dropped at least ten cents a pound.
Good harvest or bad we sank deeper in debt,
and planted more tobacco to get out,
and watched our dreams of fortune fade like smoke.

Hand-bill Distributed in Buncombe County, North Carolina: 1915

"Three years ago I owned a mountain farm,
two mules, two cows, several calves and hogs.
I raised a lot of wheat, tobacco, and corn.
Most years I did quite well, or so I thought.

But after feeding livestock through the winter,
buying children shoes, paying back
what I owed for seed and fertilizer,
I'd worked a year and hardly broken even.

I sold my stock and farm, paid off my debts,
moved my family to Eureka mill.
In that mill my fourteen year old girl
earns more than a grown man in the hills.

The mill provides you with a place to live,
coal and firewood brought right to your door.
They treat you like a king. I only wish
I'd brought my family down here years before."

If this testimony makes you want
a future working for our company,
please contact us at our Eureka Plant,
located east of Chester, South Carolina.

In a Dry Time

My crops were dying in the field.
The dog days seemed to never end.
I'd wait and curse and pray but still
nothing but the well bucket fell.
Soon it would scrape bottom.   By then
my crops would stand dead in the field.
September came in dry as hell.
The sun never blinked, no hint of a wind.
I'd pray and curse and pray but still
not even Jesus Christ could heal
dirt turned to dust, scorched roots.   By then
my crops were standing dead in the field.
I had no harvest to pay my bills.
So tried for another loan and when
the bank said sorry I begged but still
it did no good, though my eyes filled
with water, too little water to mend
broken crops dead in the field.
I left crop rows for rows of steel.

II

Mill Village

Mill houses lined both sides of every road
like boxcars on a track. They were so close
a man could piss off of his own front porch,
hit four houses if he had the wind.

Everytime your neighbors had a fight,
then made up in bed as couples do,
came home drunk, played the radio,
you knew, whether or not you wanted to.

So I bought a dimestore picture, a country scene,
built a frame and nailed it on the wall,
no people in it, just a lot of land,
stretching out behind an empty barn.

Sometimes at night if I was feeling low,
I'd stuff my ears with cotton. Then I'd stare
up at that picture like it was a window,
and I was back home listening to the farm.

But what was done was done. Before too long
the weave room jarred the hearing from my ears,
and I got used to living with a crowd.
Before too long I took the picture down.

County Fair

After the gaudy swirl of musical colors,
the hair-raising up and down voyaging,
the carnies' black-teethed testimonies,
miracles, monsters, bared flesh,
after the corn dogs, greasy french fries,
the sticky beard of cotton candy,
the gambled-for high, distant prizes,
soiled teddy bears, stroke-deadened watches,
after they spent a week's pay
for trinkets and souring stomachs, they'd end up
behind the livestock arena, these millhands
whose best dreams were crowded
only by cattle, the black dirt
of freshly-plowed fields, men who still
checked the sky like it mattered, urged here
to herd with the exiled, unribboned losers,
their backs to the stalls,
feeling the animals bump and shift
in the cigarette dark, talking little
then hardly at all, just inhaling,
not even having to close their eyes.

Low Water

In August when the dogs days came we'd check
the river in the morning and after our shift,
eyes searching for the first sign of the rock
that sprouted in midriver that time of year.

We called that rock the Colonel's Colonel. It was
the one thing in the county that bossed him.
If that rock showed three days we had it made
and knew it soon would be low water time.

That's when the water in the millrace fell.
The machines got tired as us and finally stopped.
There was nothing else that Colonel Springs could do
but let us go, at least a little while.

Out in the yard someone would play guitar.
We'd sing "Rock of Ages" or some other hymn,
or sleep until the water gained up again,
and the whistle blew and we'd have to go back in.

It was an easy time. That hour or two
made mill work tolerable. At night we'd pray
for another week of blue-sky afternoons,
at least until the drought of twenty-one.

When no rain came for a month, we thought of kin
back in the mountains praying hard as us
for crops that withered in dirt turned into dust.
Each of us praying for the other's misery.

That's when we knew the world was truly evil,
and after work we'd watch the cottonmouths
sunning on the rock we thought a savior,
taking their ease, fat come rain or drought.

Spring Fever

Each spring you knew when it was planting time.
The men would get more careless on the job
and have that far-away look in their eyes.
You'd know they were behind a mule and a plow.

They'd drink lot more whiskey that time of year,
and take a lot less from their section boss,
who like us wives knew it was the better course
to cut them slack until the fever passed.

But they were just remembering the best,
not the things they'd gladly left behind,
that made them leave. It's easy to love a life
you only have to live the good parts of.

They'd forgotten what a hailstorm does
in fifteen minutes time to six weeks work,
how long it took a hay-filled barn to burn,
when a lantern spilled its flame or lightning struck.

They'd forgotten the loneliness. The days
you wouldn't speak a word from dawn to dusk
except to cows and chickens and felt your tongue
was rusting like a plowshare in the rain.

But maybe deep inside they did remember.
They must have because every March you'd hear
men swear come planting time next spring they'd be
back in the fields. They'd say that every year.

Accident

We were running speed frames. Mary knew
those flyers could snatch your apron off or break
a bone like a twig given half a chance.
But her baby had been sick, kept her awake
three nights in a row. She was so tired
she barely kept her head up. When she did not
those flyers grabbed her hair, would not let go
until her scalp came too. I guess she screamed
though who could hear her over the machines.
I never knew a body held so much blood,
or ever wanted to know. The second hand
calmed her down enough to get her in
a car and over to the hospital.
Mary was back at work that afternoon.
She didn't want to lose a half day's wage.
After the bandages came off she wore
a wig she ordered from a catalog,
and took care not to sleep on the job again.

The Sweeper

Ma died when I was very young.
After that it wasn't long
I went into the mill to sweep,
came home for supper and for sleep.

Dad shaved my head the lint was so bad,
but I didn't cry because he said
I was the oldest child and so
must grow up faster than he'd hoped.

On winter mornings when I walked
in darkness to the mill I thought
of what Dad said and I was proud
of being a man, of helping out.

And helping other people too,
folks we made those sheets for who
still slept in sheets I helped to make,
still slept as I walked into work.

Fighting Gamecocks

Down near Broad River   we dug us a pit
a four foot deep circle   filled with sawdust
brought our best birds   well groomed and well gaffed.
We lay down our bets   the birds did the rest.

In midair they'd meet   feathers would fly.
Brought blood would stain   soak the sawdust.
Sometimes blood spilled   outside the pit
two men waving blades   weaving and slashing.

All strut and hate   their instinct to kill
pity was not   a part of their nature.
One cock would leave   that pit alive
to live a few weeks   until the next fight.

Preparing the Body

Sometimes it only took a single word.
just a look if they had drunk enough.
A hawkbill knife would flash, sometimes a gun.
The doctor closed their eyes and it was done.

That's when they'd come for me so I would walk
until I found some men out in a yard
smoking cigarettes, looking at the ground,
the women in the house with the dead man's wife.

They'd have him laid out on a cooling board,
looking like he'd passed out drunk, but then
you saw the shirt dyed crimson with his blood,
a face as white as August cotton bolls.

We'd strip the body first. The younger girls
who hadn't known a man were curious.
They might giggle, childish as the men
who'd brought us here with their little boy games.

As soon as I could get him shaved I'd leave
and wouldn't come back until a few weeks passed.
That's when she'd need the hugs, the sugared words,
some extra help with supper and the kids.

By then she'd have an inkling, not so much
of what had happened but what was to come.
By then she'd know that she would grow old young.
By then she'd know her man was the lucky one.

The Famous Photographer Visits Eureka

That Yankee photographer would stop
each time a smile or laugh slipped out.
"Be serious," he said. "This means
much more than you can understand."
I'd climb back on the stool to reach
the frame, to work more "seriously,"
while he hid behind the camera,
reduced my life to grays and blacks.

Decades later I realized why
he'd cropped the child out of that scene,
read how his photographs had changed
the labor laws across the south,
and know no one could question what
his photographs had denied me.

Revival

When Reverend Marcus Weathers pitched his tent
outside the mill to make a three-night stand
against the devil and all forms of sin,
we did our best to be there every night.

Friday evening he preached the love of God,
and all His gifts we should be thankful for,
most of all for Jesus who had shed
his blood that we might get another chance.

The second night he listed all the vices
sure to keep us outside heaven's gate,
cards and drink, dancing, fornicating,
smoking and swearing, all our other pleasures.

He saved the worst for last, as preachers will
to keep us living right. He spoke to us
of constant noise and darkness visible,
of heat worse than a July afternoon.

That's when Alec Price stood up and spoke.
He'd had a drink or two before he came.
"Forgive me if I interrupt," he said,
"but sounds to me like I'm already dead,

because that place you're talking about
is across the road, Eureka's weaving room.
After tonight I see why mill and hell
are spelled almost the same and sound alike."

We laughed that night but later there were times,
when we were sweating in that cotton mill,
we'd try out best to remember another life,
and what bad things we'd done to end up here.

III

Bearings

He's scraped manure off his boots a last time,
filled the front room with what he has chosen
to keep on owning. He's alone, his uncle gone,
gearing back through the hills unwinding into
the gasping curves and drops of the mountains.

He stands on the porch, no work until tomorrow,
millhouses planted like corn rows each way he
looks, Eureka's water tower rising above as if
a hard high-legged scarecrow. He steps down on
the strange level road, walks west toward town.

He finds a grill, asks for what he's memorized:
a hamburger and a coke and his change. Outside
in the loud afternoon he stares into windows
until he sees shoes. The clerk takes his bills
and grins when my grandfather asks for a poke.

He walks out toward Eureka's smoke and rumble,
toward the millhouses crouched and huddled in
the mill's shadow, and soon finds he is lost.
Each house might be his or maybe the next one,
and he walks an hour before he finally asks.

He tells the man he is looking for James Rash,
a friend who's just moved here. The man says,
"Tommy Singleton got fired last week. I'd bet
that's where your friend is at," and points to
a house, and so my grandfather found himself.

He stayed inside till the whistle woke him up,
and threw his boots on the roof so they might
guide him back those first evenings and later
the Saturday nights he weaved under moonshine,
searching roof after roof trying to find home.

My Grandfather Comes Calling

He was country-shy and hardly looked my way,
just stepped onto the porch and talked to Dad
about the weather, Shoeless Joe, the best
type of knife to skin a catfish with.
until Dad winked at me and went inside.

We listened to the tree frogs and the crickets
talking up a storm compared to us.
You'd thought we'd been struck dumb, hardly a word
until I said in an off-hand sort of way,
"This sure would be a nice night for a walk."

We followed the footpath down to Broad River Bridge,
leaning out into the dark, upstream
Eureka hummed, each pane of tinted glass
blue and pretty as a town-church window.
He didn't say a word, just took my hand.

Local Color

The mill shut down at twelve on Saturday,
and like so many workers he would spend
his half-day's freedom for a second wind
so he could draw the evening in a bar.

A family legend tells of one such night,
my grandmother playing rook with some girlfriends.
Like hers their husbands were out getting drunk.
They are not surprised when he staggered in.

And hardly looked up from their cards as he threaded
the doorway into the darkened bedroom,
where his hangover waited. Too soon
he'd have to deal with the morning's loud light.

They heard him yelling but no one moved at first.
They dealt the cards and hoped he'd settle down.
But halfway through the hand it just got worse.
My grandmother went to see what was wrong.

When she turned on the light he was screaming
that the devil was gnashing his body to bits.
But it wasn't the devil, just this:
his body was caught between mattress and springs.

They finally uncoiled him from the bed.
Red welts covered his chest and legs.
He thought himself a Lazarus and made
the women hear what he'd endured.

"It seemed the very jaws of hell," he said.
"It felt like ninety teeth were biting me.
The darkness smothered. I could not escape.
I thought I was dead and this was eternity."

The others just laughed, put on their coats and left.
My grandmother rubbed alcohol on the welts
while my grandfather swore he'd alter his life,
give up the drinking, go to church twice a week.

He was contrite and seemed to have changed.
He was a new man, for a few days.
But by Saturday night he was at it again.
My grandmother believed in original sin.

My Grandfather Swallows His Pride

My grandmother had the flu else she'd have gone
but she'd been in bed all day so grandfather went,
a dollar in his pocket as he walked
up to Springs' store where he unshelved salt
he thought was sugar, countered all he held,
watched the paper vanish, bluffed a math
to calculate the nickel and copper heads
the clerk had dribbled back into his hand.

My grandmother tried to get him to take it back
but he knew or thought he knew the price he'd pay,
a smirk at best, at worst a story saved
to buy a laugh at his expense. No, he drank
his coffee black all winter, into the spring,
let it scald his bitter stubborn tongue.

IV

Jokes

The best was that if Hoover ever died
and six pallbearers took him to his grave,
he'd rise up in his coffin and he'd swear
four men could do the job easily.

That joke was told in thirty-one. By then
the owners had us stretched like rubber bands,
and they would fire us if we dared complain,
and Hoover told the owners that was fine.

To have some meat on Sundays we would shoot
some gray squirrels in the woods below the mill.
We'd call them Hoover hogs, another joke
we filled our mouths with so we could go on.

The Stretch-Out

I was only seventeen, a girl
who still could trust a suit and smile.
"Let's see how fast these looms will run,"
he said, a stopwatch in his palm.

Those first night when I got back home
I swear I could hardly raise my fork.
I'd fall asleep with my clothes still on,
still weary when the whistle blew.

The child inside me felt it too,
and right then seemed to just give up.
I felt its life bleed out of me.
I cried but I cried quietly

and let the sheet slicken and stain,
so my man might lie and save what strength,
what hope a good night's rest might give.
I closed my eyes and slept again.

Flying Squadron

It was a dangerous time. From dawn to dusk
we rode from mill to mill to spread the word.
We were cursed and shouted at. Sometimes
things got more serious. We carried scars
from fists and clubs, left some friends behind
in Gaston County, down in Honea-Path,
shot by the owners' thugs or bayoneted
by frightened kids in National Guard uniforms.
At night we'd build a campfire by the road.
We'd talk and laugh and sing our union songs.
Later with a young man at our side,
we might get up and leave the campfire's glow,
find a pine straw bed to lie down on,
and prove two bodies rubbed together can
spark up heat as well. It felt so good
to breathe fresh air instead of cotton dust,
to be outside that spinning room awhile.
We knew we'd never be as brave again.

The Ballad of Elle Mae Wiggins

It was the fourteenth of September
in nineteen hundred and twenty nine,
when she made her last stand in a cottonfield
a few miles from the South Carolina line.
We won't forget the day
strikebreakers struck poor Ella Mae down.

They shot her in the chest and let her die,
then took her body into town.
She was just a linthead on this earth
but in heaven she'll wear a crown.
We won't forget the day
strikebreakers struck poor Ella Mae down.

Oh mothers tell your children this sad tale
so they will tell their children when they're grown.
She sacrificed her life to save the union.
Eureka workers, she was one of your own.
So don't forget the day
strikebreakers struck poor Ella Mae down.

1934

After the union men left town,
Old Man Springs stood by the gate.
He tried to gauge by our eyes,
unsure whose side we now were on.

As if we knew. It sounded good
what organizers promised us,
a shorter day, a better wage,
a worker getting to boss the boss.

They told us that it was our sweat
that bought the mansion Springs lived in.
The time had come to share the wealth,
they said, we've got them on the run.

But when the other mills laid off,
Spring made sure we had some work.
We'd watch warehouses fill with cloth
we knew there was no market for.

What did we owe him for those jobs?
A tough question, almost as tough
as how on earth we'd feed our kids
if strikers shut Eureka down.

When a flying squadron headed south
and crossed the Chester County line,
we left our shift to walk outside.
We filled our fists to welcome them.

Black and White

One December Colonel Springs dressed down
in overalls himself, his children and wife,
the idea being to create a Christmas card
sure to make his business partners laugh.
the chauffeur drove them to the mill, the photographer
already inside, setting up his camera.

The Colonel placed himself behind a cart
filled up with bobbins, arms taut, brow creased.
His wife stood behind him, her hair tied back
to authenticate the black look on her face.
The children too pretended they were working,
leaned their lean bodies against a machine.

The photograph turned out a shade too dark
to satisfy the photographer who blamed
a lack of proper lighting, the jolt and jar
of machinery that hurt his concentration.
But Colonel Springs was pleased and always swore
that Lewis Hine could not have done it better.

Boundaries

She thought that her beauty   bought her a way out.
She thought she could live   like she wasn't a linthead.
spend time with a man   whose hands were uncallused.

Her coat and best dress   were kept in her locker.
She'd head straight to town   when our shift had ended.
When she saw us there   she pretended she hadn't.

She would not deny us.   We took care of that
bringing men with us   to handle her beau.
We waited in shadows   until they walked by.

My sisters held her   while my hawkbill knife
stripped off her fine dress   cropped her fine hair.
Her town boy felt fists   lost most of his smile.

She understood then.   Her sweetheart did too.
Her belly still swelled.   There was no stopping that
or stopping the words   that weren't even whispered.

Some men, unmarried,   helped her make production
though none of them offered   to give her their name.
Their help was enough   more than she deserved.

V

Revenant

Below our backyards that crumbled
each day a little more
their puny allotments into
a Springmaid riverbed where
no river ran, the crosswise
laid out like coffins to bridge
a flow of forged steel,
there on those train tracks
our lives flashed before us,
rolls of Eureka gray cloth
shrouded in boxcars, leaving
Chester for Lancaster's
Grace finishing plant.
Twice a night we waked
when our millhouses rattled,
finally resettling as it
the die had been cast.

The Front

Cinderblocked a half-mile from the mill
between the First and Second Baptist Churches,
Darby's pool room, covert bar, and grill
rebuked the civic arguments of those
who claimed a hard day's work would make a man
a better, more productive citizen.

Fridays after work the men went straight
down the narrow path that led them to
the section of the village called The Front,
where no law ever came unless someone
was lying dead or leaking enough blood
he couldn't resist when cops clicked on the cuffs.

A truce was called at midnight. Numbed by drink,
men staggered home. Come morning they'd hurt worse,
scabbed, cotton-mouthed, hung over the machines,
that wailed like hungry children, wives
turning pockets out to see what was left,
a few crumpled bills, coins, mainly lint.

Breaking the Whistle

Half-sober on a Sunday, dark outside,
late February, a dreary time of year,
a mangy day-old snow lay on the ground,
we listened to Alec Price ramble on.

"To drink or not to drink," he said and held
a creek-clear pint of moonshine to the light.
"To feel bad now or later. That's our plight,
for either way that whistle blows at dawn."

"Well maybe not," said Timmy Oates. "What if
somebody took that thing apart. What a joke
to play on Springs but better still we'd get
a chance to sleep Sunday's hangover off."

"But what if we get caught," Jim Watson said,
who always was a cautious man. "We won't,"
Timmy said. "Who'd be up on that roof,
especially at twelve o'clock at night?"

We found a hammer, screwdriver, and pliers,
all the tools that Timmy said we'd need.
We drank till midnight. Then we got our coats,
and stumbled through the shadows to the mill.

The fire escape was slicker than owl shit.
Alec slipped and almost broke his arm.
We finally got up on that icy roof
and in an hour we'd taken that whistle apart.

It was after eight when they woke us up,
supervisors going door to door.
We dressed and ate and took our time before
we walked across the track and into work.

By morning break most workers knew our names.
Such things get out, but no one turned us in.
They called us heroes, linthead Robin Hoods,
who stole time from the rich to give to the poor.

Springs swore the weather knocked it down and fixed
the whistle by himself that afternoon.
Come Sunday night a guard was on the roof.
We went on home, got what sleep we could.

Brown Lung

Sometimes I'd spend the whole night coughing up
what I'd been breathing in all day at work.
I'd sleep in a chair or take a good stiff drink,
anything to get a few hours rest.

The doctor called it asthma and suggested
I find a different line of work as if
a man who had no land or education
could find himself another way to live.

For that advice I paid a half-day's wage.
Who said advice is cheap? It got so bad
each time I got a break at work I'd find
the closest window, try to catch a breath.

My foreman was a decent man who knew
I could not last much longer on that job.
He got me transferred out of the card room,
let me load the boxcars in the yard.

But even though I slept more I'd still wake
gasping for air at least one time a night,
and when I dreamed I dreamed of bumper crops
of Carolina cotton in my chest.

Plane Crash

When we heard the Colonel's son was dead
at twenty-one, burned up so bad
they had to check his dental charts
with what was left to get a match,
we first believed it wasn't true.
Such things as that were not supposed
to happen to any folks but us.
The Colonel was at work the next day
and never showed his son had died,
so we said nothing, let him pass,
glad he understood the need
for him to act like even death
could never make him one of us.

Listening to WBT

All you had to do was turn the knob
until the light clicked on and soon you'd find
rising out of static was your life.
Everytime you heard "The Weave Room Blues"
or "Cotton Mill Colic No. 3" you felt
like a deer that risked a meadow, its eyes
lifted to see the barrel too late.
Someone had caught you in his sights,
hit you solid in the guts
with all the things that you had thought
you didn't want to think too long about.
But days later you'd catch yourself
humming those lines as you worked your shift.
Maybe it was the banjo and guitar,
the way they prettied up the words,
that made those songs lighten up your heart
like a deep-water Baptist hymn.
Or maybe in the end it was the words,
the bare-assed truth making a stand
in a voice that could have been your own.

Last Interview

That's an early portrait on the wall,
painted the year I graduated from
Princeton University, the year
I took my first trip to the continent,
a disappointment, except for the wines.
But I digress. You spoke of exploitation,
the working man's abuse by men like me.
If they are so abused why don't they go
back to the farm they flee to work in mills,
became Vanderbilt Agrarians
quoting Cicero as they slop their hogs.
In thirty-four when the union leaders came
and promised everything they could, then more,
my workers stuck with me. My workers knew
I'd take care of them. Eureka ran
when other mills shut down. I took a loss
so they could have some work. Noblesse oblige
is an idea we still live by in the South.
All men created equal? Yes, perhaps
but see how soon we sort the top ones out.
Watch any group of children, they have leaders,
followers and stragglers. It does not change
as they grow older. No one questions rank
in war or politics so why not business.
Don't think that I am stupid. I see your pen
hasn't moved since this interview began.
You'll slant what I have said to fit your needs.
I know how writers work, their luxury

of always being outside looking in,
passing easy judgments while they risk
nothing of their own, mere dilettantes.
Your words mean nothing to me. I know the truth.
I gave them more than they ever had before.

Funeral

We'd known for several weeks that he was sick,
had watched him fail before our very eyes.
The doctor couldn't keep him in his bed.
He came to work until the week he died.

Two days later they shut the machinery down.
The supervisors led us off our jobs,
out to the front lawn where we formed a circle
around the Colonel's coffin, the fresh-dug ground.

The preacher read some pretty words. Then some
fat Columbia politician said
what he had come to say and it was done,
and we stood there not knowing what to do.

Some would later claim they buried him
with open eyes that he might watch us still.
For several months the night-shift workers swore
they'd seen his ghost walking around the mill.

But that was later. No one said a word
about such things as they eased his body down.
Even those who hated that old man
somehow felt empty now that he was gone.

The Colonel's son-in-law raised up his hand.
The whistle blew. "There's work to do," he said.

V

First Shift

The four-thirty whistle won't wake him this morning.
My father's awake, dreaming of paychecks.
Bedsprings creak in the other bedroom,
my grandfather coughing, my grandmother rising.
Then the clatter of pans, the warm smell of coffee,
the dog at the door, begging for scraps.

The three of them walk up the hill in the dark,
across the train train tracks, past Darby's Grill.
They pass through the gate where I cannot follow,
except in blood-memory, except in the knowledge
I eat well and I rest on the gift of their labors.

Photograph of My Parents Outside
Eureka Cotton Mill. Dated June 1950

Back against the chain-link fence,
my father's muscled left arm twists
like vine that sprouts a wire-meshed fist.
My mother leans into his chest.
She's known him a month, cannot guess
what I will see, at least not yet,
in my father's odd pose, the fingerless
awkward clutch of metal, as if
caught in a sprung-steel grip.

September, 1957

Beyond the camera's framed moment
I sit on the porch step, watch
my grandfather lean his canceled body
against the back of Alec Price's Ford.
Looming like an anchored cloud,
Eureka's water tower rises behind.

Harry Darby crouches next to a tire,
right hand knuckling the swept dirt yard.
Alec stands nearby, cross-armed,
eyes still shut thirty years later
as I watch their dead faces tense again,
remember how they came earlier that day.

"Loud enough to wake the dead,"
my grandmother hissed as fists
rattled the screen door's hinges.
They barged in uninvited,
muddied the fresh-waxed floor,
flung open the bedroom door.

and entered the darkened room
to share with my grandfather
news of their great good luck,
twenty rod-doubling rockfish
caught that morning in the tailrace
below Santee-Cooper dam.

Words finally weren't enough.
They clattered the bedpan into the corner,
tumbled sheets to the floor,
gripped wasted flesh between them—
my grandfather dragged barefoot and pajamaed
into that September afternoon.

In the dogwood tree's shallow shade
they opened the fish-gorged trunk,
worried a rainbow of flies
as they weighed and measured, recaught
each fish, argued minnows versus plugs,
sinker weights and line strength.

And stayed an hour. Fishstench
ruined the air. Slime and blood
stained the Ford. They eased
my grandmother in the backseat
when he weakened, gave him
cigarettes to bite like bullets.

And would not leave until
my grandmother acknowledged the moment,
held the green-stamp camera
against her face and glared
one-eyed at those men
who dared disturb the dying.

Tonight I hold the photograph lightward,
try to read my grandfather's face,
something more behind the cigarette,
a grimace of pain or a grin.
It is the one sure thing
I cannot remember.

July, 1949

This is what I cannot remember—
a young woman stooped in a field,
the hoe callousing in her hands,
the rows stretching out like hours.
And this woman, my mother, rising
to dust rising half a mile
up the road, the car
she has waited days for
realized in the trembling heat.

It will rust until spring, the hoe
dropped at the field's edge.
She is running toward the car,
the sandlapper relative, who spills out
coughing mountains air with lint-filled lungs,
running toward the half-filled grip
she will learn to call a suitcase.

She is dreaming another life,
young enough to believe
it can only be better—
indoor plumbing, eight-hour shifts, a man
who waits unknowing for her, a man
who cannot hear through the weave room's
roar the world's soft click,
fate's tumblers falling into place,
soft as the sound of my mother's
bare feet as she runs,
runs toward him, toward me.

Acknowledgements

The author wishes to thank the editors of the publications in which some of these poems have appeared:

America: "Drought"
Dexter Review: "Photograph of My Parents Outside Eureka Cotton Mill. Dated June 1950"
DoubleTake: "Low Water," "Tobacco"
Hellas: "Local Color"
Kennesaw Review: "September, 1957"
New Virginia Review: "Accident"
Poet Lore: "Listening to WBT"
Point: "The Front"
South Carolina Review: "Flying Squadron," "1934"
Southern Review: "Eureka"
Texas Review: "Spring Fever"
The Journal: "July, 1949"

I would like to thank the following for valuable assistance and support in the writing of this book: Bill Koon, Robert Morgan, Ann Rash, Warren Slesinger, and the National Endowment for the Arts.

DONORS

Tom and Jane Abbott
Mitch and Sarah Allen
Bob and Ruta Allen
Tom and Ceci Arthur
Robert and Susan Atkins
Susan Baker
Tom and Joan Barnet
Sam Bass
Otis Baughman
Cyndi and David Beacham
Victor and Linda
  Bilanchone
Debra Bishop
Lynne and Mark Blackman
Kathryn Brackett
Carol and Jim Bradof
Walter and Dolores Brice
David and Jessica Brown
Julia Burnett
Robert and Margaret
  Burnette
William and Katherine
  Burns
Lynne and Bill Burton
Fritz and Lori Butehorn
Jan and Toni Caldwell
Kathy and Marvin Cann
Ruth Cate and Chuck
  White
Randall and Sally
  Chambers
Bill Chidester
Victoria T. Colebank
Douglas Congdon
Rick and Sue Conner
Haidee B. Courson
Betsy Cox and Mike Curtis
Kenneth and Rachel
  Deems

Magruder H. Dent
James Drafts
Jean Dunbar
Katherine and Raymond
  Dunleavy
Alice Eberhardt
Coleman Edmunds
Susan and David Ellis
William C. and Betty
  Elston
Andy and Lynne Falatok
Elizabeth Fleming
Delie Fort
Julia Franks
Elaine T. Freeman
H. Laurence and
  Elizabeth Fritz
Carol Gallager
Laura and John Gramling
Margaret and Chip Green
Lee and Kitty Hagglund
Elizabeth Hamilton
Susan Hamilton
Benjy and Tanya Hamm
Al and Anita Hammerbeck
Jessica Handler
Monty Mullen and Julian
  Hankinson
Tom and Tracy Hannah
Robert and Carolyn
  Harbison
Darryl Harmon
Rodney and Marie Harley
John and Lou Ann Harrill
Anna Harris-Parker
Peyton and Michele Harvey
James Mark Hayes II
David and Rita Heatherly
Araceli Hernandez-Laroche

Patricia Hevener
Charlie Hodge
Richard and Janice
  Howerton
Doug and Marilyn Hubbell
Kevin and Misti Hudson
Max Hyde
Susan Hodge Irwin
Chris and Manya Jennings
Tom Johnson
Steve and Melissa Johnson
Betsy and Charles Jones
Frannie Jordan
Daniel Kahrs
Jay and Pam Kaplan
James Karegeannes
Cynthia and Keith Kelly
Deborah Kocisko
John M. Kohler, Jr.
Klaus Kolb
Mary Jane and Cecil Lanford
Jack and Kay Lawrence
Wood and Janice Lay
Francie and Lindsay Little
George and Frances Loudon
Elizabeth Lowndes
Brownlee and Julie Lowry
Julia Lyons
Gayle Magruder
Kari and Phillip Mailloux
Nancy Mandlove
Gaines H. Mason
Bill and Wendy Mayrose
Bren McClain
Betsy McGehee
Diana D. McGraw
Bill Cooper and Martin
  Meek
Molly Talbot-Metz

Larry E. Milan
Don and Mary Miles
Boyce and Carole Miller
Weston Milliken
Karen and Bob Mitchell
Laura and Scott
  Montgomery
Lynda and Bert Moore
Marsha Moore
Susan Myers
Margaret and George Nixon
Walter and Susan Novak
Cecile and Chris Nowatka
W. Keith and Louise Parris
Steve and Penni Patton
Carolyn Pennell
Terry Plumb
John and Lynne Poole
Jan and Sara Lynn Postma
L. Perrin and Kay Powell
Betty Price
Custom Products Inc.
Terry Pruitt
Eileen Rampey
Luke Perkins and Alix
  Refshauge
Elizabeth Refshauge
Ricky and Betsy
  Richardson
Anna and Charles Rickell
Laura Ringo
Rose Mary Ritchie
Elisabeth and Regis Robe
Gail Rodgers
Renee Romberger
Elena Pribyl Rush
Ellen Rutter
Cecelia and Edward S.
  Wildrick

Nayef and Premanjali
  Samhat
Tony and Kimberlee
  Sanchez
Kaye Savage
Mark and Carol Scott
George Singleton
Caroline and Ron Smith
Donna and Curtis Smith
Danny and Becky Smith
Pamela Smith
Chris Smutzer
Lee and James Snell, Jr
Eugene and Rita Spiess
Hank and Marla Steinberg
B.G. and Sandra Stephens
Tammy and David Stokes
Phillip Stone
Travis Sutton
Robert and Christine Swager
Nancy Taylor
Rick Mulkey and
  Susan Tekulve
Ray Thompson
Mary Thornton
Aaron and Kim Toler
Deno and Kathy Trakas
Lawrence and Jerri Warren
Anne Waters
Mary Ellen Wegrzyn
Peter and Kathie Weisman
Cathy and Andy Westbrook
Dave and Linda Whisnant
Karen and John B. White
William and Floride Willard
Elizabeth "Libbo" Wise
Diane Smock and Brad Wyche
Bob and Carolyn Wynn
Margaret and Mike Young

Steve and Charlotte Zides
Suzanne and Jon Zoole
John Stockwell and Diane
  Vecchio
Adrienne Z. Ables

HUB CITY
PRESS

HUB CITY PRESS is a nonprofit independent press in Spartanburg, SC that publishes well-crafted, high-quality works by new and established authors, with an emphasis on the Southern experience. We are committed to high-caliber novels, short stories, poetry, plays, memoir, and works emphasizing regional culture and history. We are particularly interested in books with a strong sense of place.

Hub City Press is an imprint of the nonprofit Hub City Writers Project, founded in 1995 to foster a sense of community through the literary arts. Our metaphor of organization purposely looks backward to the nineteenth century when Spartanburg was known as the "hub city," a place where railroads converged and departed.

RECENT HUB CITY PRESS POETRY

Rodeo in Reverse • Lindsey Alexander

Magic City Gospel • Ashley M. Jones

Wedding Pulls • J.K. Daniels

Punch • Ray McManus

Pantry • Lilah Hegnauer

Voodoo For the Other Woman • Angela Kelly

Waking • Ron Rash

Home Is Where • Kwame Dawes, editor